SANTA

S A

N T A

Text by

K A T H L E E N   P A T O N

SMITHMARK

Copyright © 1998 by SMITHMARK Publishers

SMITHMARK books are available for bulk purchase for sales promotion and premium use. For details, write or call the manager of special sales, SMITHMARK Publishers, 115 West 18th Street, New York, NY 10011.

This edition published in 1998 by SMITHMARK Publishers,
a division of U.S. Media Holdings Inc., 115 West 18th Street, New York, NY 10011.

Text: Kathleen Paton
Design: Kay Schuckhart, Blond on Pond
Editor: Kristen Schilo, Gato & Maui Productions
Art Research: Margaux King

ISBN: 0-7651-0868-2

Library of Congress Cataloging-in-Publication Data

Paton, Kathleen.
        Santa / by Kathleen Paton.
            p.   cm.
        ISBN 0-7651-0868-2 (alk. paper)
        1. Santa Claus – History.   2. Popular Culture.   I. Title.
GT4985.P365   1998
394.2663-dc21
                                                                98-21581
                                                                CIP

Printed in Hong Kong

10 9 8 7 6 5 4 3 2 1

CONTENTS

anta Claus. Just mention those two little words, and millions of people around the world immediately bring to mind an unmistakable image, that of a mirthful, very plump, white-bearded fellow just past middle age, clad in an ermine-trimmed scarlet suit, wide black belt, and heavy black boots. He's smiling, of course, proudly emphasizing his famously rosy cheeks, and he has an equally celebrated twinkle in his adorable, crinkled blue eyes.

Any school-aged child can give you the scoop on Santa Claus. He lives at the North Pole with his wife, Mrs. Claus, where they oversee a bustling toy workshop manned by legions of diligent elves. He carries a huge knapsack packed with gifts for kids. He flies

mail him a written list of what you want for Christmas. He also has the remarkable ability, during the holiday season, to appear simultaneously in scores of department stores and shopping malls, where you can tell him face-to-face just exactly what gifts you hope to find awaiting you on Christmas morning.

However, this friendly, beloved gift-bringer named Santa Claus actually began his life many centuries ago in Asia Minor, as a Christian bishop named Nicholas of Myra, who was later to become St. Nicholas. Over the ages St. Nicholas (or St. Nick, Father Christmas, Kris Kringle, and Santa Claus) was described or depicted, for example, as riding a horse or in a wagon, wearing furs or striped pants, smoking a long clay pipe, and working with a devilish sidekick with horns and a tail. Although it may be hard to believe, the jolly, familiar fellow we know today has been around for less than two hundred years.

I N T R O   D U C  T I O N

through the air in a sleigh pulled by eight reindeer, sometimes assisted by a helpful red-nosed reindeer named Rudolph, who has proven quite useful during periods of inclement weather. Santa distributes the toys to very good children by somehow squeezing his amazing girth down the chimney flue and leaving the gifts to be discovered on Christmas morning. (If your home doesn't have a chimney, don't worry—he finds other ways to get in.)

At once earthbound and supernatural, Santa sees you when you're sleeping, and knows if you've been bad or good. Though he is omniscient, it helps if you

How did a revered third-century saint end up as that decidedly secular, chubby guy at the mall? We hope that the delightful cornucopia of images to follow, presenting the evolution of Santa Claus—from his ancient origins to his special place in today's world—will help to tell the tale. And to those who lament the growing commercialism of Christmas, we might all take a lesson from Santa, who embodies the best side of Christmas: kindness, generosity, and community spirit, and who always maintains a good-natured, twinkle-in-the-eye attitude toward the whole frenzied holiday season. Or as Santa himself might say, "Ho, ho, ho!"

10

What we know about the first St. Nicholas, who was destined to become our modern-day Santa, is based mainly on legends. He is believed to have been born around 280 A.D. in the village of Patara in Asia Minor, in what is now Turkey. It is claimed that his parents, who were childless for years, were so happy to have a first-born sun that they named him Nicholas, which means "victor of the people" in Greek.

Orphaned suddenly as a teenager by a plague in Patara, Nicholas is alleged to have given his inheritance to charity and devoted himself to the study of religion. In his late

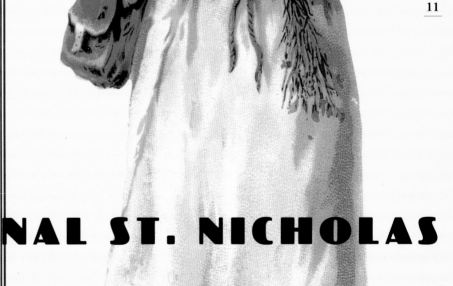

1. THE ORIGINAL ST. NICHOLAS

teens he became a priest in the still-young Christian church, and eventually was named Bishop of Myra, a city near his hometown. Because of his youth he was called the "Boy Bishop."

In medieval France, December 6th was celebrated as "Bishop Nicholas Day." A young boy would be chosen to play the "boy bishop," donning long red robes and a tall hat.

Christopher Columbus named a port in Haiti for St. Nicholas on his first voyage.

It is estimated that by the beginning of the 1500s more than 2000 monasteries, chapels, and hospitals throughout Europe were named for St. Nicholas.

The young bishop became known for his great acts of kindness and charity, inspiring people to join the growing Christian church. When he refused to bow down to the Roman Emperor Diocletian and worship him as a god, Nicholas was imprisoned for five years, but his faith remained firm. Released in 313 by the more liberal Emperor Constantine, Nicholas returned to his position as Bishop of Myra, and spent the rest of his life working for the good of the Christian church, inspiring others to convert to Christianity.

At the time of his reputed death on December 6, 343, people in Asia Minor were already relating stories about the saintly goodness of Nicholas, and were attributing miracles

hris Kringle
UND GROSSER MARSCHALL

to him. By the year 800 he was officially declared a saint by the Eastern Catholic Church. He became the special patron of children and young single women.

St. Nicholas' association with gift-giving might have its roots in a legend about him. It is claimed that he secretly aided a poor man who had three unmarried daughters by

In addition to protecting children and young single women, St. Nicholas was a busy saint! He was considered the patron of sailors, students, merchants, bankers, apothecaries, cobblers, pawnbrokers, tailors, grocers, and bakers.

tossing three bags of gold through the windows of the man's house and then sneaking away, so that the young women would have a proper dowry and could get married.

In some versions of the story the young women have hung up their stockings to dry by the fire, and the bags of gold fall into the stockings, perhaps inspiring the idea of our contemporary Christmas stockings. In other versions he has thrown the gold down the chimney.

Tales of the generosity of St. Nicholas spread from Asia Minor throughout Europe, slowly evolving into the notion of the kindly gift-bringer we celebrate today. By the end of the 1400s, Nicholas was one of the most beloved religious figures in Europe. On the eve of December 6th, St. Nicholas Day, it became the custom for children in many countries to leave out their shoes and stockings to be filled with small presents supposedly brought by the saint.

But it would still be centuries before St. Nicholas would become our own jolly Santa. St. Nick was usually depicted as a tall, thin, serious figure in floor-length red robes wearing a bishop's mitre and holding a long staff—a far cry from the rotund, apple-cheeked fellow we know today.

Wishing you Christmas Cheer

The supposed remains of St. Nicholas were stolen from Myra by a group of Italian sailors in 1087. They are now enshrined in Bari, Italy at the Church of San Nicola.

17

uring the Protestant Reformation of the mid-1500s, St. Nicholas' popularity suffered a major setback in Europe. Martin Luther said that St. Nicholas Day was a celebration "in which so much childishness and falsehood are blended." In Protestant countries the December 6th holiday celebration was moved to December 25th, and new gift-bringers were invented to take the place of dear St. Nicholas.

One gift-bringer became the Christ child himself, dress of mistletoe, ivy, or holly. Indeed, Charles Dicken's *A Christmas Carol* relied on this image as the model for the ghost of Christmas present. And France had a new visitor called *Pere Noël.*

However, in Holland the reverence for St. Nicholas continued. Tradition held that every Christmas Eve, St. Nicholas appeared on horseback, clad in the long red robes of a bishop. With him was an assistant named "Black Peter" who descended through the chimneys of children's homes and left gifts (or birch rods) around the hearth. The Dutch called the saint *Sinter Claes, Sinterklaas,* or *Sinter Claas* for short.

2. A NEW SANTA IS BORN

called *Christkindl* in Germany, who brought presents to good children on Christmas Eve. Naughtier children would awaken to find only a birch rod instead of small toys, food, or other trinkets. German children were also visited by *Weihnachtsmann* (Christmas Man). In England, another new figure was Father Christmas. He was usually depicted as a pleasure-loving fellow in a fur-lined red robe, wearing a festive head-

It was probably this version of St. Nicholas who was transplanted to America. In early nineteenth-century New York City, prominent ancestors of Dutch settlers established December 6th as the Festival of St. Nicholas. A printed woodcut made for the occasion in 1810 showed St. Nick in front of a stocking-bedecked fireplace, one stocking holding toys and fruit, and the other a wooden stick.

Another important contribution to the image of the newly emerging Santa Claus was Washington Irving. In his best-selling *History of New York,* Irving told of St. Nicholas riding over the treetops in a wagon filled with presents, popularizing the image of a new American gift-bringer as opposed to the older European one.

But it wasn't until 1822 that Clement Clarke Moore's famous poem "An Account of a Visit from St. Nicholas" clearly established a new identity for the evolving Santa. The poem, written for Moore's children, described a red-cheeked "jolly old elf" who rides through the air in a sleigh pulled by eight reindeer, places presents into the children's stockings, and returns to his sleigh via the chimney flue. Santa Claus was born!

While Santa Claus was busy emerging in the mostly Dutch and English areas of New York, another name for Santa was appearing in German-speaking America. Kris Kringle was derived from the old German *Christkindl,* the Christ child who brought presents on Christmas Eve. Eventually his name and infant image were transferred to the more popular Santa. By the late nineteenth century, the names *St. Nicholas, Kris Kringle, Father Christmas,* and *Santa Claus* had become virtually interchangeable.

The next important contribution to Santa's image came from American illustrator and political cartoonist Thomas Nast. More than any one artist before him, Nast gave Santa the attributes which are still most closely associated with him today. Beginning in the 1860s, Nast spent thirty years developing an entire story around Santa. His drawings showed a rotund, rosy-cheeked Santa in his workshop with his elves, at home, concerned about the behavior of "good" children, stuffing stockings, and surrounded by toys and a Christmas tree. Santa's typical red suit trimmed in ermine was devised by Nast, who depicted

A New York City writer in the early 1800s proposed that Santa Claus arrived on Christmas Eve from Spain, travelling in a toy-filled Dutch ship.

Kriss Kringle's Book for All Good Boys and Girls was published in Philadelphia in 1852.

Clement Clarke Moore supposedly based his notion of St. Nicholas on Wouten Van Twiller, the portly first governor of New Netherlands.

it in a book of verse about Santa's life. Through Nast's many illustrations, the Santa Claus who had begun to take shape at the beginning of the 1900s was, by the end of the century, fully formed.

And lest there be any doubts left about Santa, an eight-year-old girl was to lay them to rest in a famous letter. In the fall of 1897, Virginia Hanlon wrote to her local newspaper, *The New York Sun*, asking if there was indeed a Santa Claus. The editor who penned the printed reply, Francis Pharcellus Church, could not have known he was composing a sentence which would resound for generations. "Yes, Virginia, there is a Santa Claus," he wrote. "A thousand years from now, Virginia . . . he will continue to make glad the heart of childhood."

On December 24, 1853 in New York City, the *Santa Claus Symphony* by William Henry Fry was first performed.

Cheery CHRISTMAS

President Benjamin Harrison dressed up as Santa for his children at the White House in 1891.

In early appearances in print in America, *Santa Claus* was spelled *St Claas, Sancte Klaas, St. Aclaus, St. Iclaus,* and *St. a claus.*

During the Civil War, Abraham Lincoln asked Thomas Nast to do an illustration of Santa with the Union troops. Seeing Santa with the opposing forces was supposedly a low moment for the Confederate army.

A Visit from St. Nicholas

'Twas the night before Christmas, when all through the house
Not a creature was stirring, not even a mouse.
The stockings were hung by the chimney with care,
 In hopes that St. Nicholas soon would be there.
The children were nestled all snug in their beds,
While visions of sugar-plums danced in their heads;
And mamma in her kerchief, and I in my cap,
Had just settled our brains for a long winter's nap—
When out on the lawn there arose such a clatter
I sprang from my bed to see what was the matter.
Away to the window I flew like a flash,
Tore open the shutter, and threw up the sash.
The moon on the breast of the new-fallen snow
Gave a lustre of midday to objects below;
When what to my wondering eyes should appear
But a miniature sleigh and eight tiny reindeer,
With a little old driver, so lively and quick,
I knew in a moment it must be St. Nick!
More rapid than eagles his coursers they came,
And he whistled and shouted and called them by name.
"Now, Dasher! now Dancer! now, Prancer and Vixen!
On Comet! on, Cupid! on, Donder and Blitzen!—
To the top of the porch, to the top of the wall,
Now, dash away, dash away, dash away all!"
As dry leaves that before the wild hurricane fly,
When they meet with an obstacle mount to the sky,
So, up to the housetops the coursers they flew,
With a sleigh full of toys-and St. Nicholas, too.

And then, in a twinkling, I heard on the roof
The prancing and pawing of each little hoof.
As I drew in my head and was turning around,
Down the chimney St. Nicholas came with a bound:
He was dressed all in red from his head to his foot,
And his clothes were all tarnished with ashes and soot:
A bundle of toys he had flung on his back,
And he looked like a peddler just opening his pack
His eyes, how they twinkled! his dimples, how merry!
His cheeks were like roses, his nose like a cherry;
His droll little mouth was drawn up like a bow,
And the beard on his chin was as white as the snow.
The stump of a pipe he held tight in his teeth,
And the smoke, it encircled his head like a wreath.
He had a broad face and a little round belly
That shook, when he laughed, like a bowl full of jelly.
He was chubby and plump-a right jolly old elf:
And I laughed when I saw him, in spite of myself;
A wink of his eye, and a twist of his head,
Soon gave me to know I had nothing to dread.
He spoke not a word, but went straight to work,
And filled all the stockings: then turned with a jerk,
And laying his finger aside of his nose,
And giving a nod, up the chimney he rose.
He sprang to his sleigh, to his team gave a whistle,
And away they all flew like the down of a thistle.
But I heard him exclaim, ere they drove out of sight,
"Happy Christmas to all, and to all a good-night!"

Clement Clarke Moore

Dayton C. Fouts, is listed in the *Guinness Book of World Records* for the longest run of dressing up as Santa (1937-1997). At age 85, jolly old Fouts took his last sleigh ride to the great toy shop in the sky.

Norman Rockwell explored Christmas themes throughout his long career, and often featured Santa. This charming image was commissioned by Hallmark in the 1950s.

The practice of giving Christmas cards began in the mid 1800s. It may have originated as an easy, inexpensive replacement for the older tradition of writing holiday letters or exchanging small tokens of affection among family, friends, and acquaintances. One account claims that an Englishman, Henry Cole, commissioned an artist friend to illustrate the first Christmas card in London in 1843. The greeting, now familiar to card readers

3. VISIONS OF SANTA

everywhere, read, "A Merry Christmas and a Happy New Year to you." In America, a Christmas card said to be among the first produced was made in Albany, New York about 1851 by a merchant and engraver, Richard H. Pease. The card included an image of Santa with his sleigh and reindeer.

And why not? Santa Claus' twinkling eyes and handsome colorful attire were ripe for exploitation on the new holiday greeting cards. Just as innovative printing techniques like chromolithography made the cards colorful and attractive novelties, improved postal

service after the Civil War made it that much easier to "keep in touch" during the holidays. One hugely successful producer of the new cards in America was Louis Prang of Boston. By 1876, he was producing over 5 million cards per year. Some cards were so striking that they were hung on the Christmas tree, framed, or displayed on special stands. And Santa's jolly face was among them!

In the 1890s the mailing of Christmas postcards became popular around the world. Novelty postcards appeared, some which made Santa's eyes appear to shine when held up to a light, or pull tabs that made his head nod. Installment postcards were devised, meant to be mailed one per day and collected by the recipient like puzzle pieces, then assembled to create a complete picture. Pop-up cards also became favorites among both children and adults.

Today, generations of illustrators have continued to depict Santa Claus on greeting cards, in cartoons, and in book and magazine illustrations. But whether celebrated or obscure, the artists and illustrators who take Santa as their subject invariably bring their own styles to the comforting image of jolly old St. Nick.

Best Wishes for a happy Christmas

A merry Christmas to you

A Joyful Christmas

A DIFFERENT ST. NICHOLAS

Just as the new American St. Nick had a recognizable image and set of circumstances by the end of the 1800s, another famous St. Nicholas figure was emerging in Sweden. Artist Jenny Nyström introduced her own version of Santa around the turn of the century. Nyström's depictions of St. Nicholas were enormously popular, as they established an image of the Christmas gift-bringer that millions of people in parts of Europe grew to know and love. (Her own son was often Nyström's model for the cherubic children in her holiday paintings.) She was commissioned to create many St. Nicholas illustrations for magazines, books, and postcards.

4. SANTA AND PALS AROUN

Santa Claus obviously has his hands full at Christmas time. Luckily, he has his friendly counterparts who assist with the bringing of gifts—as well as holiday cheer—in other parts of the world. Some of them arrive by boat, riding on a horse or goat, by helicopter, or even on a surf board! Some get a jump on the season by handing out goodies around St. Nicholas Day on December 6th, while others don't arrive until the feast of the Epiphany in early January. On the next few pages is a glimpse at just a few of Santa's friends, and what they do for different holiday celebrations.

D THE WORLD

AUSTRALIA: Father Christmas and Santa Claus share Christmas duty. They sometimes arrive by helicopter or boat and join a parade to herald the beginning of the holiday season. They also can be found in New Zealand.

ENGLAND: Father Christmas (sometimes also called Santa Claus), clad in long red robes and a wreath of holly, ivy or mistletoe, arrives riding a goat or a white donkey.

DENMARK: Gift bringing is shared by tiny elfin Santas named *Julenisson*, and a Christmas Man named *Julemanten*.

FRANCE: *Père Noël* (Father Christmas), shares gift duty with *le Petit Noël*, (Little Christmas). Some say he has a devilish helper named *Père Fourchette* or *Père Fouetard*, who whips naughty children.

AUSTRIA: Santa is called *Niklaus*. He has a furry, devilish helper named *Krampus* who rattles chains and carries an empty sack. They also visit neighboring Hungary.

BELGIUM: St. Nicholas brings bags of sweets on December 6th.

CHINA: Chinese Christians hang their stockings for *Dun-che-lao-ren* (Christmas Old man), and *Lan Khoong* (Nice Old Father).

MEXICO: A Santa figure is often present when the children break the hanging clay piñatas filled with goodies. On the eve of Epiphany, the *Reyes Magos*, or Magi, fill children's shoes with small gifts.

GERMANY: *Weinachstmann* and *Christkindl* bring gifts on Christmas Eve.

GREECE: During the Christmas season St. Nicholas is honored by fishermen, who decorate their boats with blue and white lights. St. Basil brings gifts, sometimes carrying them down the chimney, on St. Basil's Day, January 1st.

GUATEMALA: The Three Kings leave gifts for children on January 5th, the eve of *al Dia de los Reyes*, the Day of the Kings.

POLAND: St. Nicholas brings gifts on December 6th.

FINLAND: Santa Claus is called *Joulupukki*. He doesn't come down the chimney in Finland, but enters through the front door gives out the presents in person.

ITALY: St. Nicholas brings gifts on December 6th. On Christmas, gift-bringing duty is shared by *Bambino Gesù*, (Baby Jesus) and *Babbo Natale* (Father Christmas). *La Befana*, a kindly old witch, brings small gifts on January 5th or 6th, for Epiphany.

JAPAN: An old man named *Hoteiosho* travels on foot and dispenses gifts from his back-pack. He has eyes on the back of his head in order to check on children's behavior.

KOREA: Santa wears a tall hat and carries his gifts in a large wicker backpack.

RUSSIA: Grandfather Frost brings gifts on Christmas Eve or on New Year's day. He wears blue instead of the traditional red. An old woman named *Babushka* also brings treats.

SWITZERLAND: Santa is called *Samichlaus*. Mountain villages are also visited by *Christkindl*, who comes on a sleigh pulled by reindeer.

PUERTO RICO: Though Santa visits, the Three Kings also bring gifts (often fruit) on January 6th. Bethlehem Day is celebrated on January 12th, with three children dressed as Wise Men leading a procession.

43

SWEDEN: St. Lucia Day, the patron saint of light, is an important Christmas season holiday celebrated on December 13th. A small bearded figure called *Tomte* or *Jultomte*, the Christmas gnome, arrives on Christmas Eve in a sleigh pulled by *Julebock*, the Christmas goat, or by reindeer.

NETHERLANDS: *Sinterklaas* arrives by ship on December 6th, then mounts his white horse and travels around the country distributing gifts.

Ethiopian: **Melkm Ganna**

Hawaiian: *Mele Kalikimaka*

German: ***Fröhliche Weihnachten***

French: *JOYEUX Noël*

Greek: **Kala Christougena**

Italian: **BUON NATALE**

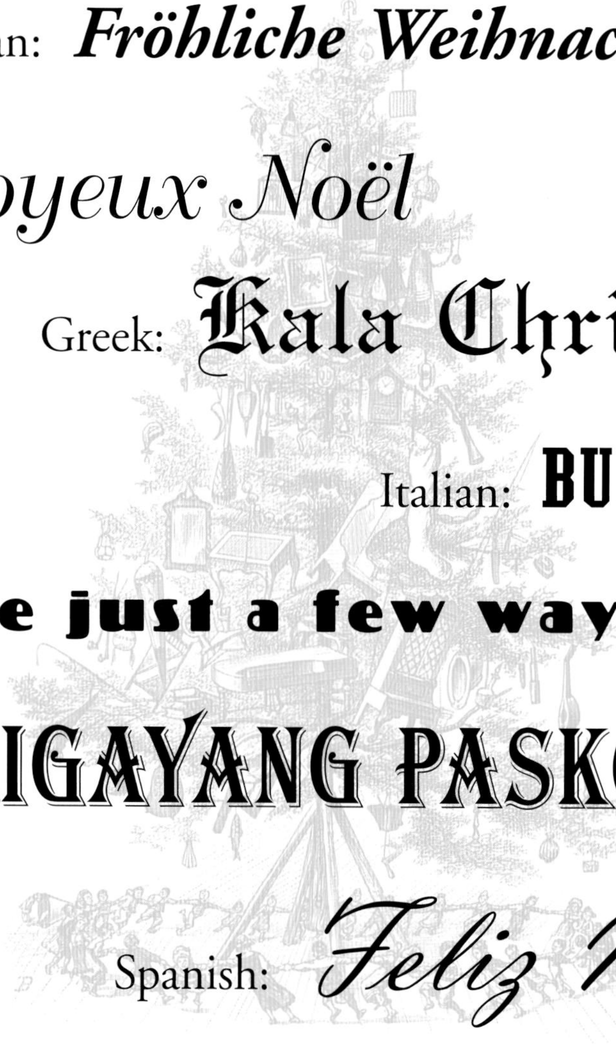

Here are just a few ways people say

Filipino: **MALIGAYANG PASKO**

Spanish: *Feliz Navidad*

Swedish: God Yul

Urdu: *Bara Din Mubarrak Ho*

"MERRY CHRISTMAS" around the world:

nce Santa's exuberant, red-cheeked face had become familiar to just about everyone, it soon became obvious that he would make a great spokesperson for loads of products and causes. For one thing, Santa represented industry. His workshop full of clever, good-natured little elves suggested a place where products (the toys) were well-made and durable, and where everyone worked tirelessly to fulfill the desires of the

turned up hawking all kinds of merchandise, from socks to candy bars. When he endorsed something it usually ended up selling.

After the success of one of the first department-store Santas, stores across the land installed a throne so that Santa could appear in person. The call for Santas became so great that in 1928, a Santa Claus school opened in Santa Claus, Indiana. Students could study such useful topics as showmanship and child psychology.

After the post-World War II baby boom, more kids than ever were ready to sit on Santa's lap and share their Christmas wishes. In fact, there were so many

SANTA GOES COMMERCIAL

consumer, in this case, millions of hopeful children. For another thing, Santa represented generosity. He was like a kindly grandfather or favorite uncle, a fun-loving guy who brought fabulous gifts, and asked nothing in return except that everyone have a great time.

In short, whether in artistic representation or in the flesh, Santa meant good business. During the first decades of the twentieth century, Santa's picture was used in advertising to such good effect that he soon

department store Santas that a retail organization in the 1950s issued behavior guidelines for them! It included admonitions not to frighten shy children with booming laughter, and always to carry tissues for kids who cried or had the sniffles.

Santa wasn't only interested in commercial profits—his high visibility lead him to work for less strictly commercial causes as well, such as raising money for charitable groups like the Salvation Army.

Illustrator Haddon Sundblom created a new Santa advertisement for Coca-Cola each Christmas from the early 1930s to the mid 1960s. The full-page ads were reproduced on the back covers of two national magazines. Sundblom's famous image of Santa picked up where Thomas Nast's left off, firmly establishing the definitive 20th-century Santa.

54

SANTA'S HOME IN THE HEARTLAND: SANTA CLAUS, INDIANA

When Santa isn't hanging out at the North Pole, you might find him in the small town of Santa Claus, Indiana. Located in the southern part of the state, not far from the Kentucky border, the town—previously called Santa Fe—was renamed in 1927. Every December the Santa Claus post office receives millions of pieces of holiday mail, which all receive the coveted Santa Claus postmark and then are rerouted to their final destinations. The thousands of children's letters that are addressed directly to Santa himself are answered by volunteers.

This otherwise quiet town, marked by a huge statue of Santa at its entrance (and which also includes Santa Claus Cemetery), is the site of one of the world's first theme parks, Santa Claus Land, built in 1946. It featured, among other exhibits, Santa's Workshop on Kriss Kringle Street.

In the 1980s Santa Claus Land expanded into Holiday World and branched out into other holiday themes besides Christmas. However, while visiting the park, one can still stay at Santa's Lodge Hotel and eat in St. Nick's Restaurant. Other area destinations include the Lake Rudolph resort and the Christmas Lake golf course.

The National Association of Professional Santas was formed in the 1930s.

The story of *"Rudolph the Red Nosed Reindeer"* was written in 1939 as a free promotional pamphlet for Montgomery Ward. It was made into a song ten years later, was recorded by Gene Autry, and sold two million copies during its first Christmas season.

CLAUS

everyone has a story

to tell about visiting Santa.

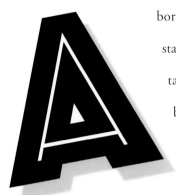A born celebrity, Santa's star quality is unmistakable, and where better to let his talents shine than on film? It's therefore not surprising that scriptwriters and directors have been inspired to depict Santa in myriad ways, from loveable hero to clownish buffoon.

One of the most beloved Christmas films of all, *Miracle on 34th Street* (facing page) explores Santa's relevance in the contemporary world. It tells the story of

CINEMATIC SANTA

Kris Kringle (played by Edmund Gwenn), a senior citizen who insists to unbelievers that he really is Santa claus. By a twist of fate he is hired to become the department store Santa at Macy's, where he preforms admirably and charms a serious little girl played by Natalie Wood. His claims to be Santa remain in doubt, however, until a bulging mail sack full of letters addressed to him is unloading during a touching courtroom scene, and the judge rules that Kris Kringle is obviously quite sane—the U.S. Post Office would never make such a mistake.

Other movies about Santa have focused on various aspects of Santa's history (*Santa Claus: The Movie*) or his difficulties (*The Christmas that Almost Wasn't* and *Santa Claus Conquers the Martians.*) Some have even exploited his wholesome image, using his familiar red costume as a disguise as Gene Hackman does in *The French Connection*, or dressing up various bad guys as Santa, as in *The Grinch Who Stole Christmas* and the

very sinister *Silent Night, Deadly Night.* In *The Santa Clause*, Tim Allen's character learns a valuable life lesson by actually turning into Santa!

One thing you can guarantee—as long as movies continue to be made, some of them will probably include a role or two (both naughty and nice) for our Santa Claus.

Featuring Santa Claus

1934 **Babes in Toyland**

1937 **Swing High, Swing Low**

1940 **Queen of the Mob**

1942 **Holiday Inn**

1945 **Road to Utopia**

1947 **Miracle on 34th Street**

1947 **The Bishop's Wife**

1951 **Double Dynamite**

1960 **The Apartment**

1964 **Santa Claus Conquers the Martians**

1964 **Rudolph the Red-Nosed Reindeer (animated)**

1966 **The Christmas That Almost Wasn't**

1971 **The French Connection**

1975 **Three Days of the Condor**

1982 **Fast Times at Ridgemont High**

1983 **A Christmas Story**

1983 **Trading Places**

1984 **Silent Night, Deadly Night**

1985 **Santa Claus: The Movie**

1986 **The Christmas Star**

1988 **Scrooged**

1990 **Home Alone**

1993 **The Nightmare Before Christmas**

1993 **Philadelphia**

1994 **The Santa Clause**

1996 **Jingle All the Way**

A *Christmas Story* wryly narrates the exploits of Ralphie, a kid growing up during the 1940s, whose sole aim is to get a Red Ryder BB gun for Christmas. A holiday favorite based on a memoir by Jean Shepherd.

Dayton C. Fouts, is listed in the *Guinness Book of World Records* for the longest run of dressing up as Santa (1937-1997). At age 85, jolly old Fouts took his last sleigh ride to the great toy shop in the sky.

SWAIN SC

Though Santa Claus remains ever faithful to good old-fashioned Christmas traditions, he is also able to change and grow with the times. For example, he usually travels in his famous bell-bedecked sleigh, but even flying reindeer sometimes need a break—in which case Santa just grabs his bag of toys and jumps into a new-fangled automobile. When he and the elves

Santa transcends boundaries. In the "global village" of today's multicultural world, Santa is likely to be of Asian, Latino, or African heritage. An equal-opportunity gift-bringer, he appears in elegant city stores, in small town shopping malls, and disadvantaged areas. "He" is usually a fellow, though he's known to be a "she" when necessary. Children don't care what size or shape (or gender) Santa comes in—they welcome St. Nick in any guise or form.

HIP ST. NICK

are too busy to answer all the Christmas mail by hand-writing letters with their old quill pens, Santa is likely to speed things up by sitting down at the typewriter. He has even been known to use a computer! In fact, Santa's adaptability to our world's changing times has made him a favorite subject on the Internet, where there are many web sites devoted to his life and work.

Whatever the future may hold in store for Santa, it is clear that he will be ready to meet any challenges, bringing hope and happiness to kids of all ages. Even if he arrives via rocket ship and has robot elves for assistants, his big bag of goodies will continue to overflow with the one gift everyone most desires: A Merry Christmas!

SANTA IN CYBERSPACE

Santa Claus prides himself on staying up-to-date with the latest technology, and the Internet is no exception. There are many web sites devoted to Santa, with more being added all the time. The sites are too numerous to list here, but if you are interested in exploring Santa on the Internet, just enter Santa Claus' name in any search engine and you'll encounter a long list of web sites where, for example, you might possibly:

❄ Receive a personal letter from Santa Claus, Mrs. Claus, Rudolph, or the elves, all postmarked from North Pole, Alaska

❄ Send your Christmas list to Santa

❄ See images of Santa Claus collectibles

❄ Get answers to frequently asked questions about Santa

❄ Learn about Santa's other gift-bringing friends around the globe

❄ Order cards featuring Santa from a cyberspace Christmas card shop

❄ Check out North Pole's weather report

SING-ALONG WITH SANTA

Santa has graciously lent his name to many holiday songs, since so many people want to sing about him! Here is a brief selection of popular song titles that feature Santa:

Jolly Old St. Nicholas
Here Comes Santa Claus
Santa Baby
Santa Bring My Baby Back to Me
Santa Claus Is Comin' to Town
Santa Claus Is Back in Town
Santa's Beard
I Saw Mommy Kissing Santa Claus
Up on the Housetop

70

SOURCES

Thank you to the authors of the folowing works:

Christmas Around the World. Dorset, England: New Orchard Editions, 1985.

Church, Francis P. *Yes, Virginia, There is a Santa Claus.* NY: Delacorte Press, 1992.

Clements, Linda. *The Spirit of Christmas: Evocative Memories of Years Gone By.* NY: Smithmark, 1996.

Giblin, James C. *The Truth About Santa Claus.* NY: Thomas Crowell, 1985.

Lankford, Mary D. *Christmas Around the World.* NY: Morrow, 1995.

Restad, Penne L. *Christmas in America.* NY: Oxford University Press, 1995.

Synder, Phillip. *December 25th: The Joys of Christmas Past.* NY: Dodd, Mead & Company, 1985.

p. 2, 56 (Inset) Private collection of Kristen Schilo
p. 3, 7, 18, 22, 29 Illustrations by Thomas Nast
p. 6 Illustration by Stephen Fay
p. 13 Archive Photos/Fotos Int'l
p. 20-21 Archive Photos/Hirz
p. 28 Archive Photos
p. 30 Illustration by Norman Rockwell, courtesy of Hallmark Fine Art Collection. A project of Hallmark Cards, Inc., Kansas City, Missouri.
p. 36, 37 Jenny Nyström
p. 38 Archive Photos/London Daily Express
p. 40- 41 Archive Photos/Irving Rosen
p. 42 Archive Photos/American Stock Photos
p. 47 Archive Photos

p. 48 Illustration by Haddon Sundblom, copyright 1960. The Coca-Cola Company. All rights reserved.
p.50-51 Archive Photos
p. 52 Illustration by Haddon Sundblom, copyright 1942. The Coca-Cola Company. All rights reserved.
p. 53 (Top) Illustration by Haddon Sundblom, copyright 1944. The Coca-Cola Company. All rights reserved.
(Bottom) Illustration by Haddon Sundblom, copyright 1940. The Coca-Cola Company. All rights reserved.
p. 56 Archive Photos
p. 57 Private collection of Kevin McDonough
p. 58 Archive Photos from *Miracle on 34th Street*

p. 60-61 Ill ustration by Ross MacDonald
p. 62 Archive Photos/Peter Billingsley, 1983 from *A Christmas Story*
p. 63 Archive Photos from *Santa Claus: The Movie*
p. 64 Illustration by John Tenniel
p. 67 Illustration by Octavio Diaz
p. 72 Illustration by Wilma Sanchez

Inger of Sweden
310 East 56th Street, Suite 11E
New York, NY 10021
Victorian paper scraps; by appointment only.